HISTORY
in a
HURRY

Victorians

written and drawn by
JOHN FARMAN

MACMILLAN
CHILDREN'S BOOKS

First published 1997 by Macmillan Children's Books
a division of Macmillan Publishers Limited
25 Eccleston Place, London SW1W 9NF
and Basingstoke

Associated companies throughout the world

ISBN 0 330 35253 9

Text and illustrations copyright © John Farman 1997

1 3 5 7 9 8 6 4 2

A CIP catalogue record for this book is available from
the British Library.

Printed and bound in Great Britain
by Mackays of Chatham plc, Kent

☞ CONTENTS

☁ OFF WE GO!

The period just before Victoria's reign had been a bit dodgy. When you're the first to do things, like having industrial revolutions (fab new inventions, etc.) it follows that you're going to feel the pinch when the rest of the world starts catching you up. In the early nineteenth century Britain was in just that position. OK, she now had a brilliant manufacturing base, with a network of canals, abundant coal and iron, and a cheap new source of energy (steam), but 'abroad' wasn't doing badly either, which resulted in tons of cheaper goods flooding onto the British market.

When Victoria was crowned in 1837 it was the beginning of a new era, probably the greatest in British history in terms of technology, invention, medicine, literature, art and telling the rest of the world where to get off. Led by a tiny little queen who, after her husband died, hardly ever went out, but who became the living, breathing figurehead of the period that was named after her. If there was ever a Top Queen award ceremony, Victoria would certainly join with Elizabeth I as one of the two greatest monarchs Britain has ever known.

But the Downside

All that's jolly nice, but it's just one side of the heavily gilded picture. Flip it over and you might see a very different image. You only have to say the word 'Victorian' and you think of gloomy, over-stuffed houses, hypocritical, holier-than-thou morality and an overbearing national self-satisfaction. It was a time when tables and chairs were covered by long drapes, because the mere glimpse of legs (*any* kind of legs) was thought to be rude. It was also a time when the very blokes that banged on and on

about morality were those same blokes who had loads and loads of mistresses, and belonged to bawdy 'gentlemen's clubs'.

And the Dosh?

Most of this new wealth that had been created went to the factory owners or their investors – the brand new, self-satisfied middle class. It certainly wasn't filtering through to the poor so and sos whose sweat and toil created it. As the century wore on the Great British Worker became increasingly pi— er... hacked off. Top communist Karl Marx noted, as he watched with bated breath in Germany, that there would either have to be some pretty heavy reforms or else dear old Britain would soon find itself all set for revolution. Read on...

Oh, by the way, if you notice a few annoying scribbles by someone called 'Ed' in this book, I'm really sorry, but it's Susie, my picky editor* – we didn't have time to change them before the book got printed.

*Just doing my job! Ed

Chapter 1

WHO DID WHAT AND WHEN: THE HISTORICAL BIT

Poor Laws

If you've ever read or watched any Charles Dickens you'll have some idea of the poverty in early Victorian times. The State, thinking it was doing the right thing (as it usually does), took responsibility for those with nothing. That was the good news. The bad news was the way they did it. The Poor Laws of 1834 made all able-bodied poor (that's me out) go to the dreaded workhouses (see chapter 5). The very word sends shivers down the spine. They made sure that these places were even less comfy than the appalling working conditions outside; they were far worse than the average modern prison. (Come to think of it, most places are much worse than the average modern prison.) Poor kids were put to work as soon as they were of any use. The poor little ba— er... baa lambs worked in coalmines, swept chimneys (from the inside), and even licked the streets clean* – anything that could bring a few more pennies into the household.

Eventually attempts were made to get things straight. In

*You're exaggerating already and it's only page 6. Ed

1838 a People's Charter was drawn up by a group who came to be known as the Chartists, and was presented to Parliament. But the wily Whigs (sort of Liberals) knew they held all the power and told them politely to go forth and multiply, imprisoning their leaders for good measure.

Pass the Spuds

Just to kick a country when it was down, God decided to give Britain a spell of atrocious weather in the mid-1840s. England's harvest was a bit of a washout, but in Ireland a million poor souls died of starvation when the potato crop (their breakfast, lunch and supper) simply didn't happen. Normally, when a country's crops fail, they get stuff in from abroad, but not us. We had terrible taxes on imported corn and other food, which had originally been set up to *protect* British farmers (the Corn Laws). These had to be chucked out pretty damn fast if the English weren't to go down the pan along with the Irish.

Vicky Gets Tough

Victoria was made queen when she was only 18 and was thus a bit of a liability to put in charge of a country, so a Lord called Melbourne, the Whig Prime Minister, was told to keep an eye on her. He was, by all accounts, quite a decent bloke (despite being a well-known child beater) and his basic job was to tell his little charge to keep her little head down and nod when told. She liked the old man and he became a bit like the father she'd never really had. But young Vicky was a stroppy little madam and soon got bored with keeping her mouth shut. She waited until Melbourne had been replaced as PM by Tory Sir

Robert Peel (who invented modern cops), before pushing her increasing weight around and propelling herself into ever deepening trub. Peel had ordered that her Ladies of the Bedchamber, who were Whig women, were to be replaced by Tory women; standard procedure when a government changed hands. Victoria stamped her tiny foot and said 'no way' (odd, I'd quite like to change *mine**) – she was sticking with what she had. Anyway, all this caused a bit of a constitutional crisis, causing Peel to resign until she rather untypically, and rather sheepishly, apologized.

Useless Fact No. 217

Victoria also managed to upset her mum, the stroppy old Duchess of York, by shoving her right up at the other end of Buckingham Palace (as far as possible from herself) whilst moving her German governess practically into her own rooms.

– YOU'RE UP THAT END MUM.

All Change
Melbourne and Peel swapped ends like tennis players; one minute one would be PM and the next, the other. Peel had, over the years, built a new Conservative party out of the ruins of the Tories, but his repeal of the Corn Laws in 1846 made him unpopular again

*I'm sure they'd like it too. Ed

with the ultra-flash landowning classes, even though it probably pleased the hungry poor no end, since they were on the verge of revolting (or being revolting)*. The Whigs came back with a bang and stayed there for nigh on twenty years, while Benjamin Disraeli built up the Conservatives yet again. None of the misery of the Irish or the discontent of the English was reflected in the Great Exhibition of 1851 however (see chapter 7), which was designed to show the world what a marvellous, happy and united nation we were.

Useless Fact No. 218

Dizzy's dad, Isaac D'Israeli, was the son of an Italian Jew, but after quarrelling with the synagogue, he had his children baptized as Christians. Lucky, really, because Jews were not allowed to sit in the House of Commons until 1858 when Disraeli changed the law.

The new man at the Foreign Office, Palmerston, had a very fiery attitude to abroad, threatening warships practically every time a British subject got into an argument. This attitude finally got him fired and he was moved sideways into the safer Home Office under Lord Aberdeen. The soon-to-be-PM, Gladstone, became Chancellor of the Exchequer. I know this is boring, but it is Rather Important.

Trouble in the Balkans

Despite all this, this government soon got Britain into a war against Russia in 1854 alongside our new mates the French, saying that we were worried about the plight of the Turks and their crumbly empire. The Russians, you see, were hitting them hard in the Balkans (ouch!). To be honest, the British didn't give a toss about the Turks, being far more worried

*Not that old joke. Ed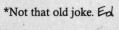

about the growing power of those dratted Ruskies. Also, by this time we were getting so cocky about our new-found wealth and power that the idea of a nice little war to teach the rest of the world not to mess with us seemed rather a laugh.

Florrie Saves the Day

The Crimean war, fought on the land round the Black Sea, was horrid and thousands of British soldiers died badly for a cause they hardly understood. The only star to come out of it was a nurse called Florence Nightingale, who kept the death score down to a lot less than it would have been without her amazing work in the disgusting field hospitals. She alone made the chauvinistic Victorian male wake up and wonder whether he'd been taking women quite seriously enough. (Not that he did anything about it.) This was the beginning of the Women's Suffrage Movement (aimed at getting women the vote), which went through late Victorian society like a dose of syrup of figs (Victorian cure for constipation).

Eventually the old Turkish (or Ottoman) Empire was mended, even though the Turks refused to behave like a proper, grown-up liberal state. Aberdeen was replaced by Palmerston in 1855, who kept the job for the next ten years.

Grease?

As soon as that war died down, the Indian army decided that they'd had enough of the English and mutinied. At the time India was firmly under Britain's ever-growing thumb, but they weren't at all wild about our filthy western ways (who is?). In fact, they weren't that fond of us at all. Part of the Indian army found out that they'd been supplied with cartridges smothered

in the grease of their sacred cow
(which we British
had been milking
successfully for
years) and the
abominable pig
(which we'd
been eating
successfully for
years). In order

SACRED! MOI?

to use them (the cartridges, not the pigs) in their rifles the
soldiers had to bite open one end to free the powder, so
naturally they went doolally (it was a bit like Christians biting
the head off – er – God) and promptly started massacring their
masters. By 1858, however, the natives stopped being restless
and did what the beastly British told them again. Phew!!

Bismarck Blusters

The Victorians loved old Palmerston (even if their Queen
didn't) but his final venture into diplomacy left him and Britain
with severe egg-on-face. Bismarck, Prussia's top minister (him
of the big moustache and pointy hat) was threatening to add
bits of Denmark to his beloved Prussia. Palmerston huffed and
puffed and did . . . nothing. Bismarck called his bluff and in
1864 went ahead, and then for an encore grabbed Austria,
effectively making Prussia all-powerful and him a real big star.
Luckily old Palmerston died before he saw these final chapters
laid out in humiliating detail.

In typical Teutonic manner, the Prussians went on to the
final of the European Domination Cup in 1871, and took the

French Empire four-nil, which might have seemed rather fab in one way (on account of we couldn't stand the French) but was a bit of a drag on the other (because we couldn't stand the Germans more)*. Eventually we had Napoleon III to stay, as he'd had his own empire whipped from under him. Actually the whole blinking business must have been pretty embarrassing for our royals, as half of them were Krauts anyway – ha ha! But it wasn't quite as bad as it sounds for Britain, because by now we had a jolly nice empire of our own to look after, consisting of 240,000,000 people who had 12,000,000 square miles to run about on.

Useless Fact No. 220

In 1876, Victoria, who'd always rather fancied being an Empress (being only Queen gets so boring), welcomed the help of arch-crawler and Liberal Disraeli (who'd replaced the now dead Palmerston and who referred to her as 'the Faery'). Together they promoted her to Empress of India by act of parliament.

The old-school Whigs died out with Prince Albert, Vicky's husband (see chapter 2), and became, under Gladstone, far more Liberal with a proper left wing. But Prime Minister Disraeli had the ear of all the moneyed folk, who certainly weren't going to lose any sleep over the amount of time democracy was taking to filter through. Why should they?

Disraeli then passed a Reform Bill which was meant to woo the votes of the poor, but they weren't fooled, because when it came right down to it, it didn't put any more food in their tummies or cash to chuck in the pub tills. They therefore kicked him out in favour of Gladstone in the autumn of 1868.

*And I can't stand your grammar. Ed

The 1867 Reforms (well, some of 'em)

- Toffs could no longer buy themselves into posh positions in the army. (That's odd, they seem to do all right now.)

- Voting was made secret. (So what? You can't eat votes.)

- Trade Unions were made legal. (About time too.)

- The Land Act went *some* way to protect tenants against their miserly landlords. (About time too – too.)

- Primary schools for all were introduced in 1870, but weren't free. (No use to kids who had to work to eat.)

- Universities were open to all. (Still no good if you were starving and had never gone to school.)

Poor Gladstone, who thought he'd done so well to get the Reforms through, got it in the neck from the moneyed classes who soon made sure that the Conservatives (and Benjy Disraeli) got back in power by 1874.

Is this getting boring? You're right. We'll move on quickly.

Here are the key dates from then on.

- **1875** Disraeli effectively buys the Suez Canal, giving Britain immense power in the Middle East.

- **1877** Disraeli then grabs a big bit of Africa for Britain from the Boers.

- **1880** Gladstone, back in power, gives it back to the Boers (very boering).

🎩 **1885** Gladstone retires in favour of Lord Salisbury, the last PM with a beard (apart from Maggie Thatcher*).

🎩 **1888** Education made free at last.

🎩 **1888** Victoria's grandson becomes Kaiser Wilhelm III of Germany (see what I mean? They're all in it together).

🎩 **1889** The two huge teams, with Germany, Austria and Italy on one side, and France and Russia on the other, start pulling very ugly faces at each other. Britain decides to stay out of it . . . for now.

🎩 **1900** Foundation of the Labour Party.

🎩 **1901** Victoria dies, and so as far as the Victorian era goes . . .

. . . that's all folks! (Well, the history bit, anyway)

*Oh honestly, even *you* can do better than that. Ed

$\mathbb{S}$— THE LITTLE QUEEN

Did you know that our gracious queen (God save her) is the great-great-granddaughter of a half-German, and the great-granddaughter of a three-quarter German? Queen Victoria's mum (Elizabeth II's great-great-grandmother) was the daughter of Francis Duke of Saxe-Coburg, a province of Germany which hardly anyone had ever heard of. To be honest, few people at the time thought the young Victoria would ever get to be queen, because a) she was a girl*, and b) there was a gaggle of more eligible guys in front of her. Luckily for her, most of them died pretty quickly, all except her rather silly uncle Willie who became William IV in 1830 – making Vicky First Reserve. Trouble was, her mum – the Duchess of Kent – couldn't stand William or his grumpy German wife, Adelaide, and vice versa, so poor little Victoria never got invited round to Windsor Castle to play with any of her royal cousins. She was, therefore, educated and trained for the throne at home by her mother, who was given £10,000 a year for the job (nice work if you can get it). At the age of eleven the Bishops of London and Lincoln were asked to examine her in scripture, history, grammar, geography, arithmetic and Latin. They reported back that she was 'fit for any task' (skydiving?).

---

*I thought all queens had once been girls. Ed

Useless Fact No. 223

Although short and already a bit on the porky side, it was thought very important that the young Victoria should carry herself like a queen. Some bright spark came up with the idea of pinning a sprig of holly to the neck of her frock so that she would keep her chin (double) held high.

Saxe Rears its Ugly Head

At that time her German rellies were turning up with great regularity and our weenie queen fell in love, or at least fancied, one of her cousins, Albert, whom she thought extremely handsome. He and his brother were a pair of princes from Saxe-Coburg (Ernest was the other one) where her mum came from. Mind you, in those days, German princes were two-a-deutschmark, so finding a free one was no big deal. Albert, being no fool, realized that young Vicky was almost certain to get queened (especially as old William seemed well ready to pop his clogs) and did little to put her off. Despite not liking England much, there was precious little for him to hang around for back home, unless he pushed brother Ernest down the castle stairs. Ernest, you see, was in line to inherit their father's run-down, second-division principality. Come to that there was more than a rumour that Albert's dad wasn't really his dad anyway but that Albert was the slip-up of his mum and a Jewish court chamberlain. This means that our present royal family could well be part German, part Austrian and part

Greek with a bit of Jewish thrown in for good measure. Doesn't leave much room for just plain British, does it*?

Teen Queen

Victoria finally became queen in 1837, when she was eighteen, and everyone in England was well-happy as they'd never really gone a bundle on King Willie and his wilful Kraut wife. Parliament even allocated £200,000 for her coronation shindig, which would be about nine million quid today (poor old William had only been given fifty grand).

Useless Fact No. 227
Directly after being crowned, Victoria left the throng (and the throne) and tore upstairs to bath her dog.

Useless Fact No. 228
The dog was a spaniel.

Useless Fact No. 229
The spaniel was called Darby.

If you've ever seen pictures of Victoria, you'll see that, despite being as pretty as a picture when a toddler, she was no oil painting later on. She was plump, with eyes like a goldfish, a permanently turned-down mouth and was very, very tiny (150 cm). Tiny but tough, however: Victoria was to stay queen for sixty-two years – an all-comers record.

To be perfectly frank, from everything I've read about her, she sounded a bit of a stuck-up little cow (well, calf, actually)

There's no such thing as plain British, anyway, so there. Ed when young. She was always going on about being bored, always complaining about her ballooning body (although she drank loads of beer and ate like a bear), and was always hiring and firing her maids as the fancy took her. If any of my female readers think I'm being unfair to pick on her frailties, you might be interested to know that she also thought that anyone who ever suggested giving women the vote should receive 'a good whipping', and that the fair sex had no place in business or any of the professions (lawyering, doctoring, etc).

"Woman would become the most hateful, heartless, and disgusting [steady on] of human beings were she to be allowed to unsex herself [sounds painful], and where would be the protection which man was intended to give the weaker sex?" said the opinionated little queen.

Albert the Nerd

Prince Albert, on the other hand, sounds to me to be a bit of a wimp – certainly when young. Being so much taller than his missus, he adopted a slight stoop, or should I say droop, and always seemed desperately anxious to please (don't you hate people like that?). The British were, to say the least, as suspicious of him as they were of *any* foreigners (at least nothing's changed there). He wasn't too thrilled about us Brits either, but probably realized on which side his German toast was buttered, so got on with it.

Worst of all, he was always cracking stupid, childish jokes which only Victoria found funny. Mind you, you've still got to go a long way to find a Kraut who makes you laugh, unless you're of the slippery banana skin school of humour**.

*What about The Oldest Profession?! Ed
**That's racist. Ed
Only joking. JF

Later in their marriage Albert became very serious and moralistic and it is thought by many that it was not so much his wife as him who was responsible for the middle-class Victorian's rapid descent into gloomy prudishness.

. . . And the Kids

The height differential between the royal pair was obviously no great problem (nudge, nudge), as they managed nine children, none of which they sent to school, because a) there'd be 'too much frivolity about' and b) her-that-must-be-obeyed 'didn't want the royal blood to be corrupted' (a damn cheek considering what a cocktail it was anyway). They therefore employed a whole posse of private tutors.

Killer Smells

Victoria and Albert were blissfully happy until the inconceivable happened. After a relatively short illness, thought to be a chill, the Prince died. What did he really die of? The clue was in the stinking cesspools round Windsor castle. Apparently when the wind was in the wrong direction the honk was horrid, and wherever there were bad smells you could bet that, lurking nearby,

WAS THAT ONE OF YOURS ALBERT?

there'd be that other scourge of Victorian times – typhoid. Poor Alfred didn't stand a chance. Lord Clarendon summed up the country's opinion of the doctors who attended the Consort: 'They are not fit to attend a sick cat.'

My Life is Over

Little Queen Victoria, aged 42, gloomily proclaimed, 'My life as a happy one is ended.' Not much on the old grammar stakes, but everyone knew what she meant. Not only did she dive into her black 'widow's weeds' but she made sure that everyone else wore black and looked miserable as well. The palace must have been a right barrel of laughs. Any dinners or balls were forbidden and, had beheading still existed, she would surely have used it to wipe the smile off anyone who dared to enjoy themselves. And this went on for years and years (and years*) with Victoria never being seen, and refusing even to collect the milk off the back doorstep. The little queen just sat for hours on end, gazing at photographs of her big dead husband.

Useless (but sad) Fact No. 231

Every night Victoria insisted that Albert's bed be turned down, his evening clothes be laid out and hot water be poured for his ablutions (spooky or what?).

Money For Nothing

Eventually the Great British Public began to wonder why they were shelling out nearly £385,000 (about 17 million in today's money) every year for an invisible queen. Victoria, sensing that the natives were getting well restless, wrote a long, pompous,

*We get the message. Ed

open letter to *The Times* (the first time before or since) the gist of which was 'Sorry, country, but gimme a break'. She eventually came out to play properly in 1887, to celebrate her 50th year as queen. Oddly enough, all was forgiven and the crowds went crazy on seeing her.

Last years

Victoria was to rule for another 13 years, during which time she became more and more crotchety. She was, however, one of the only British monarchs whose opinions were even listened to, let alone done anything about. Here are a few of her most famous thoughts:

1. She agreed with the banning of duelling and made public executions illegal. Good.

2. She opposed the shortening of working hours for women and children to ten per day. Very bad.

3. She turned a blind eye to the wretched habit of highland lairds clearing their land of crofters to make room for sheep and grouse-shooting. Very bad.

4. She refused point blank to let Ireland rule itself. Maybe good, maybe bad.

5. She began to loathe the Liberals and let everyone know it. Neither good nor bad.

6. She made Lord Salisbury apologize for calling Indians 'black men'. Very good.

7. She made it plain that she liked Scotland much better than England. No comment.*

But despite all this, Victoria reigned over one of the most remarkable periods of British history ever. One which was to

*For once. Ed

make us masters of a great empire, the manufacturing centre of the world, leaders in science and technology and feared and respected from Tokyo to Timbuktu (what went so terribly wrong? I hear you cry). But despite her mega-grumpiness, she was ever so popular with her people. On the night she died the whole population went indoors and drew their curtains. They just couldn't imagine a Britain without her. The streets were black as a bag, wet and deserted, while shops and places of amusement were boarded up. I suppose the only consolation to those of strong faith, was that she'd got her way yet again. She and her beloved Albert could now spend the rest of time together . . . presumably telling the angels to cover up their arms and legs (not to mention their wings).

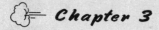 *Chapter 3*

WORKING CHILDREN –
OR
HOW THE VICTORIANS
GOT OUT OF GIVING THEIR
CHILDREN POCKET MONEY

I used to think I was really hard done by, because I had to do a paper round to bump up my pocket money. If I'd been a Victorian kid, I would have had a lot more to complain about. To make any sort of a study of them, it's important to regard the offspring of the poor as almost a separate species to those of the middle class or rich. Adult wages were so appalling (see next chapter) that kids would often have to work before their fifth birthday. Not for them any kind of education, or even playtime. If they wanted to eat, they had to work for it (quite right too).*

Employers were only too pleased to give them work. OK, they couldn't do quite much as adults, but they never gave any trouble (for fear of a severe beating) and didn't require paying nearly as much as their mums and dads (which was next to nothing anyway). There even used to be street markets in the bigger towns where the rich factory owners and landowners would hire children as and when they required them. These are some of the jobs they had to do.

*Don't start that again. Ed

Down on the Farm

It was certainly no picnic for kids in the country. Boys from a young age were used as human scarecrows, hopping around from dark till dark, scaring birds away from the fields. When older, boys and girls would be expected to do the same work as the farm labourers,

or menial but semi-skilled jobs like plaiting straw for the hat industry, crowded into small rooms and kept up to speed by horrid mistresses with canes. *But they were lucky!*

Factory Fun

At the beginning of the century, thousands of ragged young kids could be found huddled in front of the filthy, ear-splitting machines of the cotton mills of Lancashire, the potteries of Staffordshire, the nail- and brick-making factories of the Black Country or the northern steel works. Many of these kids were orphans deserted by their local parishes, whose job it should have been to look after them. They worked twelve hours a day, six days a week, practically tied to their machines but, when Sunday came at last, they were usually allowed to spend their free time... cleaning 'em. Many of the little workers were horribly killed or mangled when they fell asleep and pitched forward into the wickedly dangerous cogs, chains and levers of those early machines. *But they were lucky!*

Down Under

Up in the North, where men were men and women were grateful, whole families would work side by side in deep, scary holes in the ground, for twelve hours a day. There were no safety regulations. The younger kids would sit in dark, damp, draughty, dungeon-like tunnels hour after hour, day after day, week after week, year afte…* simply pulling strings to open the doors to let the coal trucks through. Older girls (10 or 11) were used as coal-bearers, carrying heavy loads on their backs, up and down ladders all day, while their brothers were at the coal face with the men. They, like their factory-working brothers and sisters, could also be killed – this time by rock falls, fumes or runaway coal trucks. *But they were lucky!*

Time to Climb

Just about every large house in the nineteenth century had labyrinths of chimneys that needed sweeping regularly. They used young boys forced into the sweeping biz by the poverty of their parents, or who were simply stolen by unscrupulous master-sweeps. Some, it is reported, were even sold by their mums and dads. Beware, dear readers, that's what could happen to you if you don't do your homework! Mind you, I don't know what all the fuss was about. Why use expensive, long brushes if you can get plenty of cheap, short boys? Children that resisted because of the danger of being trapped, choked or at least cut and bruised, were often goaded by sharp knives on the soles of their feet, and some even had fires lit under them if the boss thought they were taking a rest. Cruel but effective.

*Yes, yes – get on with it. Ed

I've never yet known a boy who actually went in for washing in a big way – certainly not voluntarily – but these poor mites couldn't wash either their bodies or their clothes for months on end. They soon became as black as . . . um . . . black people, and no amount of scrubbing could remove the ingrained soot. Human chimney sweeping was finally outlawed in 1870. *But they were lucky!*

Match This

The match industry was huge in Victorian Britain. In the match factories kids were used to dip the little wooden sticks into the phosphorous (used at the striking end). Absolute doddle, I bet you're thinking, compared to all that other stuff. Well, admittedly the work wasn't particularly strenuous, but it did have a couple of rather tedious side-effects. The fumes, if they didn't kill you outright, caused, at best, the rotting of all your teeth and, at worst, the disintegration of your entire jawbone (which would often lock and prevent you from eating). This was not so bad as it might seem, however, as the poor little devils didn't have much to eat anyway.* *But they were lucky!*

On the Streets

At least the kids just mentioned had some means of earning money to feed themselves. Around the streets of the big cities were thousands of youngsters who had no parents and no homes and no money (and no fun). They often – no, nearly always – fell into bad ways (just like Oliver Twist) living solely off whatever they could steal. If they didn't steal, they starved – simple. To be fair, these children did sometimes do

*You're sick. Ed

a bit of honest work, but it would only be stuff like holding the bridles of parked horses or sweeping up the horse poo so that the ladies and gentlemen wouldn't have to dirty their boots. I know what I'd have done with it (and they wouldn't have had to worry about their boots).

Most of these dreadful practices were done away with by the 1870s, largely due to the work of Sir Robert Peel and Lord Shaftesbury who gradually persuaded the great unwashed that maybe it might just might be an idea to educate their kids so that they wouldn't end up as ignorant as they were. Mind you, a fat lot of good that turned out to be until education became free.

Schools for Scoundrels

Many poor kids in early Victorian times never even saw a school (there was no law that said you had to go) because it meant their parents would have to pay. Few ever stayed at school beyond twelve anyway (stop cheering at the back!). There were some 'National' or 'British' schools run by the church but they were hopelessly crowded – a hundred pupils of all ages in one room – and the teachers were, to say the least, crappy and cane-happy. There were also the Dame Schools,

BOOKS? BOOKS?
I'LL GIVE YOU BOOKS

run by whiskery old ladies from their own front parlours. These often had no proper desks or seats, no books (rather essential in education, I'd have thought) and no computers (let alone the Internet).

Very poor children could only attend Sunday school, because they had to work in the week, but in order to go they had to be clean and tidy (there's always a catch). Easier said than sometimes done. Very, very poor children couldn't even attend these, for obvious reasons, so 'ragged schools' were set up in the very worst slums, where they could wear their ragged clothes and where they didn't have to brush their ragged hair with hairbrushes they didn't have.

Chapter 4

HOW THE OTHER HALF LIVED

The nineteenth century witnessed the birth of The Great British Middle Class (pause for fanfare). Just like a cuckoo in a sparrow's nest, it grew and became stronger year by year, until it was the most powerful force in the land. If anything, it was the uppers and middles who snuggled closer together, leaving the working and poverty-stricken classes in the cold (as usual). What separated them? What always separates people? Money, of course! And how much money did you need to be middle class? A young mid-Victorian couple were thought to be relatively safe to marry if they pulled in £500 a year (£22,000 today), and once they had reached £1000 they could be regarded as fully paid-up members of the don't-mess-with-us ruling middle class.

On the Other Hand

Briefly, just to show the comparison, a working foundryman in Derbyshire could only expect to earn £71 a year (£3,131 today) out of which he would have to support his wife and kids. And he was a skilled man. An unskilled man, like a labourer or farm worker*, could seldom make much more than £39 a year (£1,700 today) and that was only if he had steady work (which was practically impossible with a crap climate like ours).

*Or yourself. Ed

Back to the Middle

Middle-class families would usually have servants: a cook, a maid and someone to look after the kids at least. The children (there were often ten per family) hardly ever saw their parents, spending most of their time in their nursery with Nanny (didn't we all?).

Papa (pronounced *papaaar*) thought himself far too important to have anything to do with his offspring, and Mama (pronounced *mamaaar*) would probably spend all her time planning dinner parties, at the dressmaker's, or visiting friends for tea. The day-to-day bringing-up of the kids was most definitely servants' work

The only thing that dad did enjoy was the disciplining of his beloved youngsters. It was *so* nice to have a hobby. He would cane them for serious naughtiness, or make them stand in a corner or miss supper for lighter crimes. Don't go thinking that kids in those days skulked around in pure terror, however. Punishment was part of everyday life and regarded as no big deal. If you did something wrong or – more to the point – if you got *caught* doing something wrong, you got walloped. Quick, easy and fully understood. Far from being unhappy, therefore, most better-off Victorian children had rather a good time.

A Question of Taste

You either like the lush, heavy, ornate style of Victorian furniture and furnishings, or you don't. I *don't*! The buildings weren't too bad (if you're into that sort of thing) but they were mostly so over-embellished that you couldn't see the wood for the trees (architecturally speaking). The craftsmanship was truly superb, admittedly, and it puts to shame a lot of the junk they throw up these days. But so often the clean line of a bridge, arch, tower or doorway could be mucked up by unnecessary, showy-offy flounces and frills. Talking of art*, the most famous painters were called the Pre-Raphaelite Brotherhood, who tried to get back to the brilliantly lit and minutely detailed paintings of their hero, Raphael and of the other Italian artists before him. For the most part I think their stuff was over decorated and rather soppy, unless you're big on acres of angels or disrobed damsels being rescued by noble knights in woods. But then, what do I know?

Middle class Victorian houses were dark and oppressive inside, as well as outside. Weighty velvet curtains, heavily patterned wallpapers, dark sumptuous furnishings, statues, ornaments and pictures covering absolutely everything, tons of bulky over-worked furniture and a general feeling of clutter – like an antiques shop whose owner can never bear to flog anything. The whole idea, apparently, was to show the rest of the world how comfortably off they were. And, oh boy, they certainly were that.

Mamas and Papas

A big treat in those days, if you were a good child, was to be invited down to sit for a couple of hours in the evening with Mama and Papa in the drawing room (short for 'withdrawing' room, which they went to after the dining room), as it was usually one of the only areas with a huge fire. Central heating, you see, is a relatively recent invention, so those big draughty houses, with spacious hallways and lofty staircases, were often as cold as an eskimo's cat.**

*Which we weren't. Ed.
**Eskimos – or to be politically correct, Inuits – don't have cats. Ed
They do, however, have senses of humour. JF

Useless Fact No. 238
Until quite late in the century, the whole family would use the same tin bath (one at a time) which would have to be filled by the poor servants who'd trudge up and down the back stairs carrying hot jugs of large water.*

In the drawing room they would read aloud to each other from rather naff books (*I* think) like *The Water Babies* or *Black Beauty*, or even the spine-chilling writings of Charles Dickens and, a bit later, Conan Doyle (Sherlock Holmes). These last two were dead popular with the the affluent Victorians because they took the lid off how the other half – or should I say other three-quarters – lived. There's nothing like hearing about other people's misery to make your own life seem not so bad, don't you think? The Victorian middle-classes became masters at avoiding any responsibility for the poor (or even seeing them) and it could be said that their legacy has remained to this day, but maybe that's getting too political (or too boring).

Schools for the Middle Classes
The general rule for the middle classes was, boys go to school and girls stay at home to be taught by their governessessess.

*Are you sure you've got that right? *Ed*

The average Victorian middle-class girl would be tutored in sketching, playing the piano, needlework and just enough general knowledge to not appear totally stupid. Sometimes they would go on to rather snooty ladies' academies to polish their social skills – like walking upright and sitting properly (these days they simply teach you how to get out of sports cars without showing your knickers) – all for that *one* day, the pinnacle of their young lives, the reason for their existence: you've got it – marriage!

The boys went to the old grammar schools dating from Elizabeth I's day or to rip-off boarding schools usually run just to make money. Many of these were dreadful, with terrible food, awful sleeping conditions and even worse teaching. In the novel *Nicholas Nickleby*, Dickens describes the dreadful Dotheboys Hall run by the tyrannical Whackford Squeers, who got his kicks punishing the boys on a daily basis. It was not unknown for lads to be actually flogged to death in some of the worst schools (especially if their dads couldn't stump up the fees on time).

Rich Boys
The very well-off either educated their lads with private tutors or bundled them off to the big, posh and severely expensive public schools like Harrow, Eton or Rugby* (subject of *Tom Brown's Schooldays*). These too were pretty rough, tough places with lots of bullying and fagging (senior boys making slaves out of juniors) and even rioting, but they got much better as the Victorian era wore on.

*I drove past Rugby last weekend. Ed
So what? JF

School for All

In 1870 a law was passed saying that all nippers between five and thirteen *must* go to school and that their parents *must* pay something towards it. This went horribly pear-shaped with the poor. They needed reasons to spend more money like an elephant needs ballet shoes. Some even tried to con the authorities into thinking that their youngsters were dead to avoid not only the expense, but also the loss of a working member of the family. These new 'board' schools (not board-*ing* schools) were pretty primitive, but it was the very first time that working class kids got some sort of formal education. That is until the whole business became free in 1888.

Chapter 5

PUNISHING THE POOR

The Workhouse

Consider this, folks. Your family is very, very poor because neither your mum or dad can get work and there are lots of other little mouths to feed apart from your own. Unlike today, when we have social security and a whole range of hand-outs (pitiful though they still are), a family before, say, 1830 could literally starve to death without anyone giving a monkey's. With the Poor Laws, the Victorians thought they'd cracked the problem. They invented 'workhouses' as the very last option for a down and out family: the last buffer before the bitter end. Unfortunately the sadly self-satisfied Victorian middle class regarded being poor as a sin (take note Tony Blair) and sinners, as we all know, must be punished. So saying, they managed to give life to a monster rather than something that could have made their miserable brothers' and sisters' lives better. For years and years, the mere prospect of the workhouse was to terrify every poor family, and they soon came to see these cold, miserable places as the end of the line.

How They Worked

Each parish had a workhouse – a largish semi-industrial building that would house the very poorest people in the neighbourhood. The middle classes admitted that the poor needed help, but refused it unless they came *into* the workhouse. In return the 'sturdy beggars' (as they were referred to) or able-bodied poor (that lets me out!) would be required to work on whatever might benefit the parish. These grim establishments were, almost unbelievably, designed to be *more* uncomfortable than the lowest level of survival in the outside world. That's charity for you. To be honest, it was probably to make sure that nobody tried to go there thinking it was like some kind of free slap-up hotel. Husbands were separated from wives and both (as well as the kids) were made to wear uniforms just to make them feel even more rotten. Orphan children (and there were loads) were sent to special

orphanages, very like workhouses, where they were often starved and beaten by corrupt and sadistic house matrons. The food in all these awful places was like the very worst kind of school dinners, and designed to be just enough to keep the inmates alive.

Apart from all that, the workhouses were rather nice.*

Chapter 6

AWAY-DAYS...
VICTORIAN STYLE

The Victorians really went overboard on the idea of the coast as *the* place for holidays. To be honest, up till that time, even the *idea* of a holiday for anyone but the very rich seemed a bit like prisoners being allowed to go to the pub, but the new middle classes had the loot and were sure gonna spend it. You've only got take a look at the architecture of most of the bigger resorts – all those icing sugar hotels, ornate piers, wrought iron shelters and painted railings along the promenades – to realize that the nineteenth century was when it *all* happened. It was most definitely the golden age of the Great British Seaside.

For Mr and Mrs Victorian and the littl'uns, the summer holiday became the most important fortnight of the year. From

early June to late August, loads of mighty steam trains could be seen and heard snaking out of the stonking steel and glass cathedrals that were the new London stations. They'd huff and puff their way down to towns like Brighton or Weymouth, or from northern stations to Blackpool or Scarborough, chock-full of excited Victorian families; fathers resplendent in striped blazers and straw boaters, mothers and daughters in their fanciest frocks and little boys in soppy miniature sailor suits. In those months, there was seldom a room to be had, or more than a square yard (metres hadn't been imported yet) of free beach to be found at any of the resorts that ringed Britain.

Those at the posher end of society, not wishing to mix with the hoi polloi, would rent a house by the sea and transport their whole family, servants, pets and all, for a month at a time. Those at the bottom end seldom got out of their gloomy industrial towns or run-down villages, because either their beastly bosses wouldn't allow them the time off work, or they simply couldn't drum up the surplus cash (I know how they felt).

The Day Trip

Towards the end of the century, however, things got a little easier for the poor poor and the private railway companies (pre-nationalization), realizing there was money in them there beaches (and them there workers), advertised cheap day-trips to places like Margate, Southend or Skeggy (Skegness). Once there they'd travel in charabancs (brightly painted carts with rows of seats) pulled at a leisurely pace by pairs of strong horses. As only the rich could afford restaurants (cafés hadn't been invented yet), the punters would have to take everything

they needed for the day – food, drink, parasols, children, etc. –
in large wicker baskets.

No Flesh Please We're British

When they got to the sand or pebbles, the Victorian trippers
didn't slip into skimpy, clingy bikinis or revealing trunks like
we do now, but preferred to stay fully dressed, lace-up boots
and all. They had this thing about revealing their bodies, you
see, so if they did decide to swim, they would use bizarre
bathing machines: daft horse-drawn huts on wheels that were
dragged down to the water's edge just to make it difficult for
any passing peeping
Toms to sneak
a view of a
bare leg

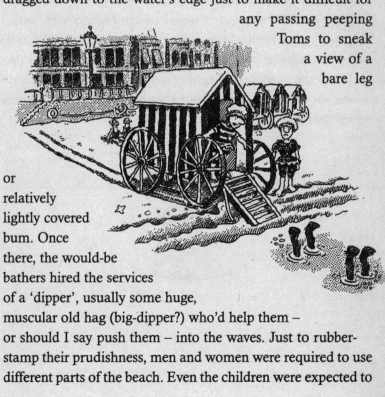

or
relatively
lightly covered
bum. Once
there, the would-be
bathers hired the services
of a 'dipper', usually some huge,
muscular old hag (big-dipper?) who'd help them –
or should I say push them – into the waves. Just to rubber-
stamp their prudishness, men and women were required to use
different parts of the beach. Even the children were expected to

stay fully dressed, but, if lucky, were allowed to take their shoes and socks off (big deal).

Seaside Fun

It was at this time that all the good old spectacularly British institutions like the donkey ride, Punch and Judy shows, candyfloss, and pink rock candy (with the name of the resort running through it) came into their own. The pier was also a *must*, for as well as all the normal stuff like fortune tellers, penny slot machines, distorting mirrors, or those big paintings of fat ladies that you put your head through, there were the end of pier shows. These were troupes of entertainers who would sing and dance to the ditties of the day like 'Oh I do like to be beside the seaside', or 'Daisy, Daisy, give me your answer do'. Then for the tired and oft-times tipsy tripper, it would be back to the sooty suburbs, tired but happy and no doubt humming saucy seaside songs.

Chapter 7

TIME TO SHOW OFF: THE GREAT EXHIBITION

Once upon a time Britain led the world in trade, technology and science.* Prince Albert, who'd begun to show signs of being one of us, wanted the rest of those foreigners to know just who and what they were dealing with (typically German). Nobody, including our now ramshackle and under-trained army, was that keen on *another* war – too expensive (and anyway we might lose). 'How's about an exhibition?' cried Albert. Not *any* old exhibition – the biggest and bestest the world had ever seen. What did he call it? The Great Exhibition, of course. It was to be a huge display of everything the world could produce and each and every country was invited to exhibit their best stuff free of charge. Behind it all was the knowledge that when it came right down to it, it would be a nifty way of letting the rest of the world know that Britain was Best.

We were becoming very rich by flogging our new-fangled technology all around the globe. In the Midlands and oop north the dark satanic factories and mills were churning out loads of flash gear that was being snapped up as quickly as it was made. But if you read the earlier chapters you'll see that a lot of this prosperity was only a sham – the masses of British workers had never been poorer and they could only look on miserably as the middle classes prepared to show off their new-found success and loot for the world to see.

*We know, you've already told us. Ed

Where and What?

There was a big competition to design the building to put everything in. Prince Albert had always been rather fond of greenhouses and conservatories and thought it might be rather a whiz to build the biggest greenhouse ever seen. He therefore went for a plan sent in by Joseph Paxton (there were 233 others*) which was basically a mighty glass palace (the area of four footie pitches); easy to put up, and even easier to take down. It was to be called the Crystal Palace. They decided to plonk it bang in the middle of London's Hyde Park (it was moved to south London the following year), despite the objections of the terribly sniffy residents of Kensington, Mayfair and Belgravia, who liked to ride their horses there and no doubt cavort in the bushes (without their horses). To save chopping down ancient trees, they simply built around them.

*233 Joseph Paxtons, eh? Ed

Useless Fact No. 252
The lavs at the Great Exhibition were the first public ones in the whole world. Before that you probably had to go before you went (if you get my drift).

Oh No You Don't
The objections to the exhibition were fabulous. The mad-as-a-snake King of Hanover said that no foreigner would dare visit the damn thing because Londoners were such a dangerous bunch of cut-throats (we still are, by all accounts). Others said that the whole construction would blow down in high winds or be smashed by hailstones and some cheery souls even reckoned that putting all those people under one roof would set off another plague. But there were some severe and justified worries over the safety of the Queen and her prince, as there had been many, albeit fairly weedy, attempts on their lives.

Useless Fact No. 253
One of the only problems they had was to come from all the birds that found their way into the exhibition (without paying). Why the problem? Use your imagination. The doddery old Duke of Wellington suggested sparrowhawks, and as soon as one was brought through the door, all the little birds flocked off.

The Exhibition opened in 1851 and was truly fab: real steam locomotives, futuristic houses for the workers (sadly, for the far-distant future), massive working steam machines, models of new bridges, handicrafts and artefacts, diamonds and precious stones from the colonies, carvings in ice and coal – all in all 14,000 exhibits and surprise, surprise, more than half of 'em British.

Useless Fact No. 255
Among the exhibits presented was the French Commissioner's walking stick, entered under the subsection 'Machines for the Propagation of Direct Motion'. When challenged, it was relocated under subsection 'Objects for Personal Use'. Another walking stick, designed for lame doctors, contained test tubes and an enema (ask your teacher).

It was only open for 140 days, but during that time 6 million visitors came from all over the world. Schweppes, who did the catering, got through a fantastic million bath buns, 32,000 quarts of cream, 33 tons of ham and 113 tons of other meats (redundant sparrowhawks?).

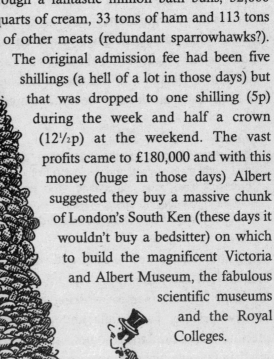

The original admission fee had been five shillings (a hell of a lot in those days) but that was dropped to one shilling (5p) during the week and half a crown (12½p) at the weekend. The vast profits came to £180,000 and with this money (huge in those days) Albert suggested they buy a massive chunk of London's South Ken (these days it wouldn't buy a bedsitter) on which to build the magnificent Victoria and Albert Museum, the fabulous scientific museums and the Royal Colleges.

Chapter 8

VICTORIAN SCIENCE

The Victorian era was probably most remembered for the amazing advances in science and technology*. Every day must have seemed like Christmas to the better-off British. For a start, in not much more than half a century they were to witness a complete transformation in transport and communication. All those rickety old stagecoaches (and their no longer needed horses) had been scrapped in favour of the brill new railway network, whose spidery fingers had begun to cover the whole country. Also, there was a new system of canals, which meant that goods could be transported far more easily than had been possible by road (no doubt using the old, redundant horses to pull the barges). Not only that, but the new-fangled electric telegraph meant that by using coded signals a message could be received at the moment it was sent, which was a mind-blowing concept to a people used to a still-shaky postal service. Not only that, but by 1866 they could even talk to abroad in the same way.

Scientifically Speaking

Ever since the Voltaic Pile (ouch!), a primitive battery, had been invented in 1800, scientists were tripping over each other to find more uses for electricity. By the end of the century, the shell-shocked Victorians could turn night into day at the flick of a switch, chat to their distant rellies without leaving their

*That's the third time you've told us that. Ed

front rooms, use motors that didn't have to have coal fed to them on a regular basis and listen to music without having a symphony orchestra in the parlour.

Science as a job had at last become 'respectable', and big companies suddenly saw the pot of gold at the end of what had seemed a very expensive rainbow. Scientists, you see, only became 'scientists' in 1883. Up till that time they'd been called 'Natural Philosophers' which, you must admit, sounds a bit of a mouthful.

By the end of the Victorian era Britain could take the credit for:
Thecanopener,thelightbulb,thesteamship,thewireless,ele
ctricity,matches,anilinedyes,plastics,shampoo,theelectric
motor,thethermosflask,cheapsteel,thetorpedo,trafficligh
ts,blowuptyres,blowupdolls*,Meccano,thevacuumclean
er,thebicycle,thesteamlocomotive,theomnibus,fingerprin
ting,thelawnmower,theelkectricclock,tonicwater . . .
and much, much more.

At the Doctor's
By the end of the 19th century Britain was becoming quite a good place to be ill. At last medical scientists were getting a grip on how our bodies actually worked. Best of all was the discovery of a satisfactory way of putting a patient to sleep while having his insides pulled out. Alcohol, which had been used until then, had been sort of OK, but it usually took the

*Ibetyouthoughtyoucouldsneakthatonein. Ed

patients too long to get pi— inebriated (try me, try me!), and sometimes had a rather nasty side-effect – like killing 'em. It was the dentists who discovered the answer by suggesting the breathing in of ether, chloroform or nitrous oxide (which was quite a laugh). Best of all, the infamous 'germs' (unlike the infamous Germans) were rooted out and found responsible for most of the diseases around at the time. Thanks to Frenchman Louis Pasteur, they even found a way of immunizing the population *against* them.

In 1865 Joseph Lister discovered that by scrubbing down everything in the operating theatre with antiseptic soap (carbolic), deaths could be reduced by 30%, and later surgeons discovered that rubber gloves were also quite useful in the battle against lurking infection (and kept their hands soft when washing up).

The pinnacle of this age of discovery came a couple of years after Victoria's death, when a married couple called the Curies, again in France, discovered radiation as a method of zapping cancer. Fat lot of good it did them: Pierre Curie got himself run over by a lorry and poor Marie, his wife, died of the very thing she'd been trying to cur(i)e.*

*That is the very worst joke in this book. *Ed*

Chapter 9

YOU GOTTA PICK A POCKET OR TWO

One of the downsides of having a large percentage of the community near starvation (and a small percentage most definitely not) is that you tend to get quite a lot of antisocial behaviour (like poor people trying to nick the rich people's stuff). Funny that! Never was this more true than in early Victorian times. In the big cities especially, thieving was a way of life (does this sound familiar?). To get some idea of how it all worked in London, read *Oliver Twist* (or, if you can't be bothered, get the video).

London Life

Next time you're in the big city, try walking through the back streets between the Embankment and, say, Shaftesbury Avenue. It's still just about possible (providing you ignore the mobile phones and yuppy wine bars) to get some sense of the rabbit warren of gloomy streets that teemed with low-life in the nineteenth century. Tenement upon tenement of cheap rooming houses (called rookeries) that made even the seediest of today's inner-city areas look like Zurich High Street. Rough families sleeping even rougher in doorways (Government, take note), splashed by the carriages of the upper classes as they whooshed past on their way to the music halls, restaurants, gambling houses (and brothels)*.

*Careful . . . Ed

Crime, you see, was basically a class thing; poor people stole from the rich to stay alive, and the thefts were mostly not worth writing home about. Unlike today, anyone outside the working class who did something naughty was shunned by his mates and regarded as a rotten egg or a bounder: as a result there was much less fraud and big city jiggery-pokery.

Useless Fact No. 269

It's interesting to note that Barings Bank – the one that went bottom-up due to the dirty dealings of one Nick Leeson (he lost them 800 million quid) a couple of years ago – was no stranger to fraud. Back in the 1850s a chap called William Smith embezzled money from Barings because he'd got into financial deep water. Hoping to avoid a scandal, they gave him £150 to settle his debts. I bet young Leeson wished they'd done that for him.

. . . and Drugs?

Since everything from opium to cocaine to cannabis to heroin to sherbert dabs was legal and used on an everyday basis there was no real need for dodgy drug dealers. None of those flash carriages with blacked-out windows careering round the streets like we see today.

Useless Fact No. 274

Rumour has it that Queen Victoria was a heavy user of cocaine* and laudanum (opium in wine) and had it delivered to the palace just like we have milk (or used to).

In the early 1830s it was calculated that there were as many as 115,000 people living on what they could nick either to eat or to sell. And that was just in London! There were organized Fagin-type gangs (anything up to 100-strong), highway robbers and, would you believe, river pirates (doesn't that sound brilliant?).

Visiting the Natives

Sensational writers of the time would often employ what turned out to be the forerunners of policemen to go with them into the very roughest and poorest areas ('Angel Meadow' in Manchester or 'China' in Merthyr Tydfil, for instance).

It was as if they were explorers diving into the deepest, remotest jungles, just so that they could sell their slightly jazzed-up accounts of daring to the tabloid equivalents of *The Sun* and *The Star*, or the 'Penny Dreadfuls' (the hugely popular little papers that specialized in 'orrible murders described in the most grizzly detail).

Useless Fact No. 275

One such intrepid explorer described a trip down the Thames to see a bare-knuckle boxing match as 'A Day's Pleasure with the Criminal Classes'. Patronizing or what?!

*I really think you ought to mention that such drugs were used for medical reasons. Ed

Takes all Sorts

A typically middle class Victorian sociologist (people studier) called Mayhew wrote an 80-page report for the *Morning Chronicle*, in which he concluded that:

1. Criminals are idle and vagabond (not the good ones – they're busy and rich!*).
2. Pickpockets rarely drink (it would impair their niftiness).
3. Young thieves spend whatever they earn on low prostitutes. (What's a 'high' one?)
4. The 'street people' can be recognized by their 'high cheekbones and protruding jaws' and their 'hatred of continuous labour'. (Gosh! Does that make me a criminal?).

Strangely enough, a school teacher reporting on a visit to the infamous debtors' prison, Newgate, also described the prisoners as having features 'strongly marked with animal propensities' (charming), and that many of the younger ones looked like monkeys

THERE'S SOME GUY GOIN' ROUND WHO SEZ WE LOOK LIKE MONKEYS

(isn't that monkeyist?). L. Gordon Rylands, another blasted sociologist, worried about the lawbreakers' ability to reproduce themselves faster than 'respectable' people, seriously suggested that they should all be taken off the streets and killed. (Crikey, L. Gordon, I'm always glad to see someone taking the bull by the horns, but what would you have done about my parking tickets?) He went on to give a

*There is no such thing as a 'good criminal'. Ed

breakdown of all the different kinds of thieves, numbering over a hundred in all. Under the heading of 'Sneaksmen' – 'those that plunder by means of stealth' – he listed the following:

- **Till Friskers:** those who ransack the tills of shopkeepers while they're looking the other way.

- **Sawney Hunters:** those who nick bacon and cheese from cheesemongers' shop-doors (obviously not Jewish or Moslem) (or should that be Muslim?).

- **Noisy-Racket Men:** those who steal china from outside china shops.

- **Dead Lurkers:** those who pinch coats and umbrellas from passages at dusk, or on Sunday afternoons(?).

- **Snow Gatherers:** those that pinch washing off lines.

And more generally –

- **Gonolphs:** street thieves

- **Swell Mobs:** professional pickpockets.

Useless Fact No. 286

A professional handkerchief thief would have to pinch between 20 and 30 a week to be able to support himself.

Captive Audience

Mumming was another way of extracting money in Victorian Britain. No, it wasn't the kidnapping and exploiting of mothers, but a strange practice of men and boys who blacked up their faces, broke into respectable houses and performed plays *at* the owners before demanding money. Blimey, I thought the Gilbert and Sullivan musicals of the time, or our very own Andrew 'Lord' Webbers, were daylight robbery, but surely that must be going too far to get an audience.

Most amazing of all was that Mayhew said that none of these professionals ever went outside their own little area of crime. It's nice to see a real specialist, I suppose.*

Social reformers and churchmen, who usually can be relied upon to miss *any* point, blamed the huge amount of crime on a lack of moral training and education, but anyone with half a brain realized that if all you did was educate them, you'd just as likely end up simply with better educated criminals. Golly, they might even get *better* at it. I mean, try lecturing some destitute so-and-so with a life expectancy of only 35 years (which was that of the poorer Victorians) about the wages of sin, when they were the only wages they could possibly hope for.

Useless Fact No. 299

The biggest killer in those days, by the way, was tuberculosis, otherwise known as 'the Captain of the Men of Death' or 'the White Plague', which took one third of all poor men, women and children.

Crime in the Country

Poaching always has been and always will be part of country life and as such was never treated as *proper* crime. But in the 19th century large gangs came from the towns and did it *properly* (or, should I say, carried it out on a much larger scale). For instance, some clever chaps murdered horses and then offered to buy the carcasses off the distraught owners for dog

*What is it that *you're* good at, Mr Farman? Ed

food (try that down the pony club), while gangs of sheep stealers and cattle rustlers would often be seen knocking on butchers' back doors providing 'hot' meat for the urban market.

Another dead popular countryside crime was setting fire to things (arson-about). Anyone with the slightest grievance against anyone else would simply torch his fields, his barns, his wife, his mother-in-law or worse (or better!).

Animal Crackers

Animals were often maimed to settle arguments (a trifle unfair methinks). Some gullible stable lads even tried 'horse-magic' (passed down from would-be witches) to make their masters' horses the finest and best groomed, but often ended up killing them (the horses, not the masters).

Useless Fact No. 333

Talking of witchcraft, three women were sentenced to hard labour in 1848 for opening up the body of a living cat with scissors, taking out its heart, sticking pins in it (the heart that is) and then burying it in the earth. Apparently they had nothing against their miserable moggy, but were using it as a method of getting back their lovers (what about cat lovers, I say).

Poor Crimes

Many of the crimes seem rather petty by today's standards but nicking from your boss to make ends meet (or simply to stay alive) was dead common. Here are some of the dead commoner crimes.

- Gleaning: the picking up of loose ears of corn after the harvest. (How despicable!)

Wood Stealing: cutting wood off trees to make a fire for the home. (Deeply horrendous!)

 Nailing: the nicking of anything from metal hinges or latches to agricultural implements (combine harvesters?) to make into nails. By the mid-19th century there were over 40,000 men, women and children making nails or supplying dodgy metal to the factories.

 Corving: the practice of putting huge bits of coal with loads of space in between in the bottom of containers called 'corves', and then sprinkling the top with smaller bits to make it look as if the corve was densely packed. Most miners were on 'corve-work': that is, they were paid by the number they filled. (Makes sense, if you ask me!)

 Bugging: the substitution by hatters of a cheaper cloth than the one shown to the customer.

 Dock Pilfering: the arrival of dockers for work in the morning looking skinny, but leaving fat. This wasn't due to a hearty lunch but to an elaborate system of nets and strings under their coats to carry all manner of goods. A lot of ship equipment and food disappeared this way and was sold to local grocers and storekeepers (and those wretched nailmakers).

 Bobbing: watering down the milk and selling the surplus. (Blimey, these days people go out of their way to get watery or skimmed milk.)

Pawnography

Pawnbrokers (or 'Leaving Shops' or 'Dolly Shops') are one of the last relics of Victorian city life to survive today. The poor would, and still do, 'pawn' (semi-sell) their possessions (for a fraction of their worth) towards the end of the week when the wages ran out, on condition that they could buy them back on pay day. If they didn't have the dosh and therefore couldn't reclaim them, the pawnbroker could sell the goods for whatever he could get.

One of the most popular crimes of the day was to rush round to the pawnbrokers with nicked gear, claim it was yours, and walk away with the loot. That being said, many pawnbrokers were receivers of stolen goods anyway. Nice little business, eh?*

Girly Crime

In 1857 only 27% of crime was committed by women and by 1900 it was down to 18%. It has to be said that by far the greatest cause for women to end up in court was prostitution, which was all the rage in a hypocritical society that hid its in-house sexuality under a thick blanket of respectability. These poor women were regarded as the female half of the criminal classes and shunned in public for letting down their sex (?). However, the respectable Victorian male often thought differently . . . but never admitted it.

It is interesting to note that the upmarket brothels where the respectable Victorian males were to be found, were completely ignored by the police (who were no doubt using them themselves).

*That's just what you would say. Ed

Useless Fact No. 342

Sleepy old Ipswich, when it was a 19th century garrison town, was known to have 53 brothels. That must be one a week (and one spare)*.

As for crimes against common prostitutes – no worries. It was generally regarded that anything that happened to a woman who sold her body for money was fair game. It wasn't till Jack the Ripper and Thomas Neill Cream began doing them in a little too often that any real attention was paid.

Why So Many?

It doesn't take Claire Rayner to work out why prostitution was top of the pops among poor women. With so many orphans, so much indescribable poverty, such miserable wages and, much more to the point, no Social Security, it was often a choice between that or the workhouse. Having read about the workhouse, which would you choose?

*Trust you to work that out. Ed

Chapter 10

JUST DESSERTS

At the turn of the century (1800) punishment was deeply severe and deeply unfair. One could be punished almost as severely for nicking a man's pocket handkerchief as for killing him (you might just as well kill him and then nick it). It was a time when a farm worker could expect to receive three months' hard labour for taking a couple of children home to feed his starving turnips*. Prisons were no fun and absurdly corrupt (nothing's changed there). The habit of stumping up cash to pay your jailer a discharge fee in order to be to allowed to leave, had just ended. Crikey, with our prisons threatening to go privatized, it all seems to be going full circle.

Foreign Holidays

The other popular punishment, lasting long into the 19th century, was the sending of naughty people on long 'working holidays' to the penal colonies in Australia and America. The lucky prisoners were often kept on 'hulks', dreadful old rotting ships parked way offshore to prevent escape, for anything up to two years before the great trip to the New World.

Useless Fact No. 353

It seems incredible, but in the year of our Lord 1997 the government are seriously considering bringing back prison ships as a way of finding cheap accommodation for the rocketing number of offenders.

*I think you've got that slightly wrong. Ed

Sometimes transportation was regarded as a bit of a result, and far from being a warning to others it was reported (unreliably) that some chaps actually committed crimes in order to get a free trip to, as one wit put it, 'somewhere with a wonderful climate, to one of the finest regions of the earth, where demand for human labour is every hour increasing, and where it is highly probable you may ultimately gain your character and improve your future.' Others claimed that conditions in the penal settlements were not fit for animals (except kangaroos) and many perished from the worst slave labour. All this stuff features in Charles Dickens' brill book/movie/vid: *Great Expectations*.

Pentonville Prison in London was one of the other places that you might be sent before transportation. There you'd be kept in solitary confinement for anything up to two years with nothing but a bible for entertainment (Oh Lord!) and, when moved around the prison (to be whipped and stuff), you'd be made to wear a mask so you wouldn't be recognized (and this was only two lifetimes ago).

Labour Prisons

Some prisons, in the early half of the century, required the inmates to do daft tasks during their visit (sounds like school, eh?). Some would be required to walk a treadmill all day (which doesn't sound quite so crazy when you consider that some people pay good money to run nowhere on running machines at poncy fitness centres). Others would be required to turn a stiff hand-crank connected to nothing (see Pointless Things to do in Victorian Times). Even worse, other poor devils simply shifted cannonballs all day, from point A to point

B and then back again, which, you must admit, doesn't sound like a great deal of fun. All these punishments, plus little bonuses from boot, lash or fist, were completely up to the jailer (and what side of the bed he crawled out from that day).

Later in the century, they were allowed to do such super things as pick tarry old ropes to pieces day in and day out, to provide 'oakum', which was used to fill the cracks in ships' hulls. Beats shifting cannonballs, I suppose.

Useless Fact No. 359

'Galvanizing' was a punishment for prisoners who looked to be taking things a bit easy. This was the administering of the new-fangled electricity (which they were still looking for other uses for) in shock form. Ouch!

Ticket-of-Leave

If a prisoner was noted for good behaviour he was made a 'ticket-of-leave' man. This meant he was given a conditional pardon and could finish his sentence early. So far so good, but unfortunately these men found it impossible to get work and usually finished up as professional 'garotters'. Garotting was all the rage in mid-Victorian times and involved throttling someone whilst robbing 'em. In the criminal fraternity, garotting was regarded as quite a science (no doubt studied 'Inside'). It became such a craze (like roller-blading) amongst muggers that it brought about the Garotters Act in 1862, which made fifty lashes a cheeky little addition to any sentence for armed or violent robbery.

Useless Fact No. 366

The death sentence for anything apart from murder was only dropped in 1861 and the last public execution was in 1868. All public hangings had been at Tyburn, now Marble Arch (sounds more fun than Speakers' Corner!), but in 1783 they moved the event to the appalling Newgate Prison which was only pulled down in 1902.

WOULD YOU MIND HANGIN' AROUND SOMEWHERE ELSE?

Pictures not Prisons

The first national penitentiary, the largest prison in Europe, was at Millbank and cost an unheard-of £450,000. Although that one is now no more (you can find yourself trapped in the Tate Gallery instead*), many of the prisons like Wandsworth, Parkhurst and the aforementioned Pentonville are still going strong, which is regarded as well out of order by many prison reformers. These prisons, which admittedly seem a little – how should we say? – old-fashioned these days, were regarded at the time as the bees' knees by prison reformers like John Howard and Elizabeth Fry. Today, most of them house tons more prisoners than they were ever designed for.

*Philistine! Ed

Hard Up?

Debtors' prisons, like Marshalsea (as featured in Dicken's *Little Dorrit*) were extraordinary places. Dickens' own father had been imprisoned there in 1824, and his son's descriptions almost defy belief. It was a complex of rat-infested alleyways, completely cut off by high walls from the rest of Southwark in London, where it was situated. Inmates had rooms, and some even had servants, according to wealth and status, but all food and comforts had to be brought in by their families. If the family was really destitute they would move in with the prisoner, as did Dickens with his dad. The conditions that prisoners lived in were in direct proportion to how much they could pay the warders (sounds fair). The Marshalsea was finally closed five years after Victoria was crowned.

Useless Fact No. 367

Perhaps because it was so near the river, the Marshalsea was a very popular place for banging up pirates (proper ones, not just river ones).

Although prisons still left a lot to be desired at the end of the Victorian era, it must be said that they were an absolute holiday compared to those of a century earlier. Even so, they were still all about punishment and had nothing whatsoever to do with rehabilitation (nothing's changed there then, I see*). Having said that, the Victorian era features high in the league of prison reform – but, like many other areas of Victorian society, there sure was a lot to reform.

*Been 'inside', then, have you? Ed

TIME'S UP

Well, that's the Victorians finished with – I've used up all my words. I'd be the first to admit that as a mighty book of reference mine's a bit shortish. What do you expect for the price of a pint?* Having said that, I bet you know a little more than you did when you started, and with a bit of luck you might even want to find some other books on the subject.

On the other hand, if you're anything like me, you'll be anxious to get on to something else. While casting around for a particular 'something else' why not try another book in this series? Please make sure you don't get through them too quickly though, as you might overtake me and have to write the blasted things yourself.

*I hope that your readers will have no idea what a pint costs. Ed

Other

HISTORY
in a
HURRY

books by John Farman

Ancient
Egypt

Tudors

Vikings